Who? Me?

A Millionaire At 40?

A Rags to Riches Story

Made in Singapore

Elaine Robertson

Author's Note
The events depicted in this book are based on real-life experiences. The characters' names have been changed to protect their identity.

This book is dedicated to Mrs Yu.

Thank You for entrusting me with your story

**A millionaire
is somebody with a net worth of at least
USD $1 million.**

It's a simple math formula based on one's net worth. When what one owns (your assets) minus what one owe (your liabilities) equals more than a million dollars, you're a millionaire.

Table of contents

Foreword

Embarking on this literary venture with the Yu family unveiled a narrative not just of individual triumph but of a collective journey through adversity, resilience, and an extraordinary financial strategy that defied norms. This story, at its core, is about how Mrs Yu accumulated the wealth required for both Mr and Mrs Yu to retire before she turned 40. Their story raises poignant questions about the financial logistics that underpin such a life-changing decision as Ms. Yu's bold move in 2017, when she chose to leave her flourishing career behind, dedicating herself entirely to her children's well-being and education, first relocating to the Philippines, then to the UK.

Yu's post-retirement life paints a picture of unanticipated prosperity, marked by frequent holidays, the acquisition of UK property sight unseen, and a lifestyle that seemed unburdened by financial constraints. This narrative seemed almost mythical to me, a British observer, accustomed to the Pound Sterling's dominance. Yu's financial freedom, especially post-migration to the UK where they immersed themselves in volunteer work, stood in stark contrast to common narratives of financial struggle and immigrant hustle. Their ability to live so lavishly, seemingly retired in their 40s, challenged my preconceived notions about wealth and its geographical ties, particularly considering Singapore's historical context as a former British colony in Southeast Asia, a region often underestimated in its potential for generating such substantial wealth.

Upon my initial meeting with the Yus, their youthful demeanor and apparent lack of financial worries intrigued me deeply. My curiosity, fueled by both my British directness and a genuine interest in their story, led me to delve into the origins of their wealth. Through a series of candid conversations, primarily guided by Ms. Yu's openness and my investigative inclinations, a fascinating narrative unfolded. Ms. Yu, herself surprised by her financial status before the age of 40, revealed a story of strategic decisions, resilience, and perhaps a touch of serendipity, all underpinned by a strong faith in divine providence. Her journey to millionaire status was not just a personal achievement but a divine move to provide her children with alternatives to the rigid expectations of the Singaporean education system.

The title of this book, "Who? Me? A Millionaire Before 40?" reflects the astonishment and humility with which Ms. Yu regards her financial success. Her story is a testament to the unexpected paths life can take as she was born into humble beginnings; the granddaughter of a fisherman and an insurance agent. The daughter of one who did not even complete his primary school education. It challenges the reader to reconsider preconceived notions about wealth, success, and the geographic and cultural factors that influence them. This narrative goes beyond a simple account of financial acquisition; it's a deeper exploration of a family's love, sacrifice, and their faith in God.

Introduction

In the bustling city-state of Singapore, a place renowned for its remarkable transition from a modest trading post to a global financial hub, the story of Ms. Yu emerges as a beacon of inspiration and a testament to the power of resilience and strategic foresight. Born in the late 1970s, during a period of rapid industrialization and economic growth, Ms. Yu's journey from humble beginnings to becoming a self-made millionaire before the age of 40 is a narrative that mirrors the ambitions and dreams of many in this vibrant metropolis.

Singapore, with its unique blend of cultures, rigorous education system, and competitive economy, provides a backdrop that is both challenging and nurturing. Ms. Yu's early life, marked by the typical pressures of academic excellence and societal expectations, laid the foundation for her relentless pursuit of success.

This memoir delves deep into the heart of Ms. Yu's experiences, exploring the nuances of entrepreneurship in a city where the distinction between success and failure can be razor-thin. Through her eyes, we witness the transformation of Singapore into one of the world's wealthiest nations, a transformation that is not just economic but deeply social and cultural. Her story is a reflection of this metamorphosis, embodying the spirit of innovation and the relentless pursuit of excellence that characterizes this nation.

Yet, Ms. Yu's journey is not just a tale of financial success; it is a narrative rich with lessons on perseverance, adaptability, and the importance of maintaining one's integrity amidst the pressures of wealth and recognition. It offers insights into the challenges of balancing personal life with the demands of a burgeoning career, the significance of mentorship and networking, and the pivotal moments that can change the course of one's life.

As we unfold the chapters of Ms. Yu's life, we encounter a diverse cast of characters—mentors who believed in her potential, adversaries who challenged her resolve, and a supportive community that played a crucial role in her ventures. Each interaction provides a layer of depth to her story, showcasing the importance of human connection in the journey to success.

Moreover, this memoir serves as a mirror reflecting the societal values and dynamics of Singapore, examining how culture, family, and education shape the aspirations and approaches of individuals navigating the path to success. It poses critical questions about the nature of ambition, the ethics of business, and the true meaning of wealth, encouraging readers to ponder their definitions of success and fulfillment.

In chronicling Ms. Yu's ascent to millionaire status, this book also explores the broader theme of what it means to be a self-made individual in a society that is both meritocratic and fiercely competitive. It highlights the juxtaposition between the collective ethos of Singaporean society and the individualistic drive required to stand out and achieve extraordinary levels of success.

This extended introduction sets the stage for a biography that is not only a personal account of triumph over adversity but also a commentary on the societal, economic, and cultural forces at play in one of the most dynamic regions of the world. As readers embark on this journey with Ms. Yu, they are invited to reflect on their own ambitions, challenges, and the values that guide them through life's uncertainties.

Through the lens of Ms. Yu's remarkable story, this book aims to inspire, educate, and provoke thought, offering a multifaceted exploration of success in the modern age. It is a story of determination, innovation, and the indomitable human spirit, resonating with anyone who dreams of making their mark on the world.

As we navigate the chapters of Ms. Yu's life, we are not just following the trajectory of a self-made millionaire; we are witnessing the evolution of a soul shaped by its experiences, a mind sharpened by challenges, and a heart enriched by the journey. This is the essence of Ms. Yu's story—a narrative that transcends the boundaries of individual achievement to touch upon universal themes of growth, resilience, and the enduring quest for meaning in our lives.

Chapter 01:
Roots of Resilience: The Chan Legacy

In the heart of Singapore, within the vibrant tapestry of its diverse cultures, was born Ms. Yu—a beacon of ambition and resilience, a third-generation Singaporean of Chinese descent. Her entry into the world marked the beginning of a journey for her young parents, Mr. and Mrs. Chan, who at the tender ages of 25 and 23, respectively, found their lives forever changed. United by their faith, having met in the serene ambiance of their local church, they embarked on the daunting yet exhilarating adventure of parenthood.

The Chans were emblematic of hard work and perseverance; neither boasted academic accolades, yet they were steadfast in their dedication to their careers. Mr. Chan's days were consumed by the physical demands of his labor in the bustling shipyards of Singapore, a testament to the city-state's maritime legacy, before transitioning to the burgeoning oil tools sector. Mrs. Chan, equally industrious, committed her working life to the manual intricacies of the pharmaceutical industry, contributing to the health and well-being of the community.

Together, they made a solemn vow, under the watchful eyes of their faith, to dedicate their lives to the upbringing of Ms. Yu—their cherished firstborn. In her, they saw not just a child, but a divine gift, an embodiment of their love and a symbol of their hopes. Financial stability was an elusive dream for the young couple, yet they remained undeterred, pledging every ounce of their hard-earned resources to provide for Ms. Yu. This commitment was not borne out of obligation but was a heartfelt dedication to the one child they believed was preordained for them by a higher power.

The narrative of the Chan family is one of modest beginnings, unwavering faith, and an unrelenting work ethic. It is a story that mirrors the broader saga of many Singaporean families, navigating the complexities of life in a rapidly evolving city-state. Ms. Yu's journey from this humble background, under the guardianship of her devoted parents, laid the foundation for a future where she would transcend the limitations of her environment to carve her own path to success.

Chapter 02:
High Above, Grounded in Tradition

Nestled among the urban canyons of Singapore's high-rise landscape, Ms. Yu's formative years unfolded in an abode perched on the 17th floor, a vantage point that offered her a bird's-eye view of the city's pulsating life. This flat, high above the ground, was not just a structure of concrete but a cradle of familial warmth and tradition, housing an extended family that included her doting parents, Mr. and Mrs. Chan, the venerable Grandpa and Grandma Chan, and a kind-hearted extended family member from Setiawan, Malaysia who ensured the smooth running of the household.

In this vertical community, where the sky seemed within reach, Ms. Yu's childhood was steeped in the rich aromas and flavors of Cantonese cuisine, courtesy of Grandma Chan, a culinary maestro whose skills were whispered about in awe. The kitchen, under Grandma Chan's domain, was a magical place where traditional dishes were conjured, serving as the heart of their home. Despite her native tongue being Cantonese, Grandma Chan chose Mandarin when speaking to Ms. Yu, a decision that laid the early foundations for Ms. Yu's bilingual abilities. This was a precious gift, considering the linguistic duality that Singapore's educational system celebrated.

The linguistic landscape of Ms. Yu's upbringing was further diversified as Grandpa Chan spoke only English! English became the lingua franca of the household, bridging generations and cultures under one roof. This early exposure to a multilingual environment was not just about communication; it was an immersion in a cultural mosaic, preparing Ms. Yu for a world where adaptability and understanding would become her strengths.

Only the lowest and middle class in Singapore lived 'among the clouds'. The wealthy lived in houses built on land in land- scarce Singapore. Ms. Yu's life was a blend of modernity and tradition, innovation and heritage, set against the backdrop of a rapidly developing Singapore. Her humble beginnings were the foundation upon which she would build her future.

Chapter 03:
Shadows and Legacies

In the woven tapestry of Ms. Yu's childhood, Grandpa Chan emerged as a figure of complex influence, his life story a testament to the era's turbulence and his own personal trials. His youth, marked by aspirations of medicine, was abruptly halted by the chaos of World War II, altering his life's path and setting him on a journey far from the halls of healing he had envisioned. Fluent in English and with a penchant for the eloquence of the BBC, Grandpa Chan was a man of contrasts, born into wealth yet embittered by the vicissitudes of fate.

His parents, affluent owners of vast rubber plantations in Setiawan, Perak, led lives of leisure that seemed untouched by the concerns of the common man. Yet, it was in mid-life that Grandpa Chan found a new calling in the realm of insurance, where his endeavors brought him considerable success. His marriage to Grandma Chan, a woman of resilience who had faced abandonment, was orchestrated by familial hands. She brought 3 children from her previous marriage into her new marriage. She was the woman who washed his parent's clothes! One can only wonder how she engineered a marriage to a man who stood to inherit much wealth! Surely, he could have deserved a virgin of his own social status. According to family gossip, Great-Grandma Chan ordered Grandpa Chan to marry Grandma! How very strange! They went on to have 4 more children in their long union.

Ms. Yu's relationship with her grandfather was marred by his incessant habit of smoking cigarettes and the shadows of his cynicism towards Christianity—a stark contrast to the faith that guided her own life. Grandpa Chan's disdain for the religion was rooted in a betrayal long past in the church of his youth (a priest had run away with church funds), coloring his worldview and casting a pall over his interactions with his granddaughter. Yet, it was his relentless emphasis on education and success that ignited a fire within Ms. Yu, a desire to transcend expectations and carve her own path.

Despite the ambivalence that marked their relationship, the undercurrent of his influence was undeniable, pushing her towards achievements that were fueled by a mixture of defiance and a deep-seated need for approval.

This narrative thread of Ms. Yu's life, intertwined with Grandpa Chan's complex legacy, illustrates the intricate dance of familial relationships and personal growth. It is a story of contrasts—of aspirations thwarted and then reimagined, of bitterness juxtaposed with resilience, and of the indelible impact of one generation upon the next.

Chapter 04:
Chosen Families

Amid the bustling life of the Chan household, Grandma Chan pursued her own passions, reveling in the camaraderie and strategy of mahjong, a game that brought her joy and a much-valued social life. She also had too many grandchildren to care for. Left without much choice, as Mr and Mrs Chan had to work at their jobs, they left Ms. Yu in the care of a dedicated nanny on the weekdays, fostering an arrangement that would deeply shape her childhood.

Ms. Yu found a second home with the Lee family, where she spent her weekdays enveloped in a warmth and affection distinct from that of her own familial bonds. The Lee household was vibrant and loving, with three older "sisters" who embraced Ms. Yu as one of their own, filling her days with laughter, attention, and the unique joy of being part of a larger sibling group. Their home became a stage for Ms. Yu, where she delighted in performing song and dance routines, especially enamored with the melodies of Liu Wen Zheng, her performances met with enthusiastic applause and encouragement from her nanny's family.

This unique arrangement, born out of necessity and sustained by genuine affection, became a cornerstone of Ms. Yu's upbringing, weaving into her life a tapestry of experiences that spoke to the complexities of love, family, and resilience. Mrs. Lee, in particular, found solace and purpose in her role as Ms. Yu's nanny, the presence of this bright, young soul offering a balm to the challenges of her own life. The bond forged in those formative years remained unbreakable, a testament to the enduring power of chosen families and the unexpected ways in which we find and give support.

Chapter 05:
Doorway to the World

Within the humble confines of a 12-story building, nestled amidst the vibrant heart of Singapore, young Ms. Yu found a realm of wonder at the doorstep of Mrs. Lee's home. Seated there, with a bowl of macaroni soup cradled in her hands, she became a familiar fixture to the passing neighbors, her innocent gaze and big eyes unlike that of typical Chinese drawing smiles and warm greetings from all who passed by. Many often didn't think Ms Yu was fully Chinese as she did not have fully Chinese features. She always looked slightly Eurasian to onlookers. This doorway, a portal to the world beyond, offered Ms. Yu a panoramic view of life's tapestry, sparking an innate curiosity that mirrored that of Mrs. Lee, the matriarch of her weekday refuge.

Mrs. Lee, a vivacious spirit with a penchant for community and connection, became Ms. Yu's unwitting mentor in the art of social navigation. Together, they traversed the local market's bustling lanes, where Ms. Yu absorbed the nuances of human interaction, her young mind cataloging every exchange, every snippet of conversation with the keen interest of a budding social savant.

Amid these daily adventures, a seemingly mundane moment transformed into a lasting memory. As Mrs. Lee attended to Ms. Yu following a meal, a stubborn speck caught her eye—a nascent mole that would etch itself into Ms. Yu's identity. It was situated just towards the right edge of Mrs Yu's lips. In Chinese culture, such marks are laden with meaning, and Ms. Yu's was no exception, heralding a life of never knowing hunger, of tasting the world's delicacies. This mole, a small yet profound marker, became a symbol of Ms. Yu's journey through life, a journey flavored by the richness of experiences, the sweetness of connections, and the spice of curiosity, all savored from the doorway of her youth.

Chapter 06:
Early Echoes: Melodies and Early Matriarchs

At merely five years of age, the musical world welcomed Ms. Yu with open arms as her mother, Mrs. Chan, introduced her to piano lessons. Like a natural, Ms. Yu embraced the piano, her innate talent for music and performance shining brightly, bringing joy and delight to all who witnessed her blossoming skills. She quickly became the adored "Little Princess" of her family, her performances an embodiment of both joy and precocity. Her father affectionately dubbed her "Little Professor," a nod to her remarkable intellect and early achievements in both the arts and academics. Ms. Yu's journey through her early education was marked by effortless success, a testament to her sharp mind and diverse talents.

This period of her life also illuminated the influential figures around her, particularly the youthful aunts and uncles on the cusp of their own life stories. Among these figures, Aunt Maisy stood out; her path was dramatically altered by the educational opportunities provided by Grandpa Chan, leading to an international love story and a life of comfort and style, admired by Ms. Yu. Yet, Aunt Maisy's privileged life and demanding nature during her brief return to Singapore for her wedding left a complex impression, blending awe with the stark realities of familial dynamics and expectations.

After Aunt Maisy's grand wedding, she embarked on a new chapter in Canada, leaving behind the intricate tapestry of her Singaporean roots. Her absence, punctuated only by her return for Grandpa Chan's eventual funeral, painted a poignant picture of distance and detachment.

This chapter of familial history was not lost on Ms. Yu, who observed the nuanced interplay between financial generosity and personal affection. Aunt Maisy's life, with its illustrious education and international romance, became a canvas against which Ms. Yu would paint her own aspirations, albeit with a mindful approach to the lessons of independence and financial wisdom.

In contrast, Aunt Lauren's journey offered a different kind of inspiration. Embodied in her was the spirit of self-sufficiency and hard work, traits that resonated deeply with Ms. Yu. Aunt Lauren, who tread her own path with determination, illuminated another aspect of life's possibilities for Ms. Yu—showing her that ambition and independence could coalesce into a life rich with personal achievements. Her skills in nursing and clairvoyance, particularly the palm reading that forecasted a life of unexpected turns and frequent travels for Ms. Yu, sowed seeds of curiosity and wonder in the young girl's heart. These prophecies, though initially met with disbelief, eventually unfurled a tapestry of dreams for Ms. Yu, dreams of exploration, discovery, and the forging of her own destiny.

The paths of Aunts Maisy and Lauren sketched a broad spectrum of life's potentials, framing Ms. Yu's early impressions of what it meant to carve one's path in the world. From Aunt Maisy's tale, she gleaned the complexities of familial support, as Grandpa Chan seemingly practised favouritism; giving his youngest daughter opportunities denied to her elder siblings. From Aunt Lauren, she learned of resilience, the beauty of charting one's course without the safety net of familial wealth. These narratives, rich with lessons and latent with future aspirations, nurtured in Ms. Yu a resolve to not only meet but exceed the benchmarks set before her. They instilled in her a drive to navigate life's myriad pathways with wisdom, courage, and an unwavering belief in her own capabilities.

The departure of Aunt Maisy and Aunt Lauren to Canada marked a pivotal moment in Ms. Yu's young life, expanding her world view beyond the immediate familiarity of Singaporean life. Their transition from Singaporean to Canadian citizens underscored a broader narrative of migration and identity, themes that resonated deeply with Ms. Yu as she navigated her own place within her family and society.

Chapter 07:
Anchors of Resilience

Aunt Christine, Mrs Chan's sister, emerged as a pillar of strength and selflessness amidst the family dynamics. Her dedication to education and her sacrifices for her siblings set a profound example for Ms. Yu, embodying the virtues of familial loyalty and personal sacrifice. Aunt Christine was probably the brightest of all 11 siblings; but she gave up pursuing her dreams of further education, choosing instead to work as a teacher to feed her younger siblings and supplement the family income.

Each Christmas, as Aunt Christine presented Ms. Yu with a new board game, it was not just a gift but a symbol of the love and support that underpinned their family's bond. These moments of connection and celebration became beacons of light for Ms. Yu, guiding her through the complexities of her upbringing.

The story of Mrs. Chan's family of origin, rooted in the island of Pulau Bukom, offered a glimpse into a way of life that was rapidly disappearing in the face of Singapore's modernization. Mrs Chan's father was a humble fisherman. The government sold the entire island to Shell Oil Company so that they could build an oil refinery on it. The resettlement to Queenstown, while a step into the future, also represented a loss of a connection to their ancestral livelihood. This narrative of transition, from the simplicity of island life to the structured existence in public housing, mirrored the broader transformations within Singaporean society.

Mrs Chan was able to complete her compulsory 10-year education because of the move from the island to the mainland of Singapore. Previously, seeking education meant taking a boat from the island to the mainland followed by a bus ride. The whole journey would probably have taken her 2 hours just to get to school in the mornings and another 2 hours for the trek home. It was no wonder she hardly went to school in her primary years! But things improved when Mrs Chan moved to the mainland of Singapore.

Mr. Chan, with his unyielding work ethic and loyalty to his family, stood as a testament to the values that propelled Ms. Yu forward. His life, characterized by hard labor and devotion, was a constant reminder of the dignity in perseverance and the integrity of keeping one's commitments. Ms. Yu's observations of her parents' marriage, grounded in mutual respect and unspoken sacrifices, became a foundational element of her understanding of relationships and personal integrity.

As Ms. Yu grew, so did her awareness of the disparities and challenges within her extended family. The juxtaposition of Aunt Maisy's privileged existence against the backdrop of her grandparents' and parents' more modest lives highlighted the varied paths one could take in life. It instilled in her a determination to forge her own destiny, informed by the lessons of her elders but driven by her own aspirations and dreams.

Through the years, as Ms. Yu navigated her academic and personal growth, the stories of her family, their struggles, triumphs, and the quiet sacrifices that stitched their lives together remained a constant source of inspiration and motivation. She learned the value of resilience in the face of adversity, the importance of education as a tool for empowerment, and the strength that lies in familial bonds and cultural heritage.

Chapter 08:
With Loving Hearts and Joyous Song

Amid the high-rise dwellings that sketch the skyline of Singapore, Ms. Yu's childhood unfolded, rich with the companionship of her cousin Sheryl. Nestled within the same towering block, their homes were not just physical spaces but realms of infinite possibilities where imagination reigned supreme. Sheryl, only two years Ms. Yu's junior, became more than a cousin; she was a confidante, a partner in every escapade, a witness to every dream whispered under the canopy of stars visible from their urban vantage point.

Their days were a symphony of laughter and music, their voices mingling in song, their feet moving in harmony to rhythms only they could understand. Ms. Yu, with her natural leadership, guided their play with the confidence of someone born to lead, her decisions shaping their activities with a blend of authority and irresistible charm. This dynamic, reflective of Ms. Yu's inherent qualities, found a later echo in the spirited nature of her son, Peter, whose youthful exuberance and assertiveness brought back memories of her own childhood leadership.

The trajectory of Ms. Yu's life took a defining turn with her initiation into formal education. The legacy of her nanny's influence, a testament to the power of mentorship and guidance outside one's immediate family, paved the way for Ms. Yu's entrance into one of the nation's most prestigious state-owned all-girl schools. It was the school of choice for the wealthy.

However, the Chans and Mrs Lee weren't wealthy. They were far from wealthy. This institution, steeped in tradition and excellence, was not just a school but a gateway to a world of opportunities, a place where the futures of its students were sculpted with precision and care.

All public education in Singapore was and still is, free of school fees. One only had to pay for uniforms, books, and food had to be bought from the vendors who sold within the school.

The decision, influenced heavily by Mrs. Lee's insistence and Mrs. Chan's compliance, was more than an educational choice; it was a commitment to a trajectory that promised distinction and success. Mrs. Lee, leveraging her connections and employing persuasive charm, ensured Ms. Yu's place within the hallowed halls of a school renowned for molding women of caliber and substance. Mrs Lee's very own children had attended this school, celebrated in popular culture for its illustrious alumni, symbolized not just academic rigor but the shaping of future leaders, visionaries, and trailblazers. Some of its alumni included the wife of the reigning Prime Minister; Mrs Lee Kuan Yew, just to name a few. Here is where the daughters of scions of Singapore society get an education.

The school was situated in Singapore's premier district. In the 1980s, unless you had some form of privately owned transport, one wouldn't venture far in search of schooling. The school was situated 15 minutes by transport from Mrs Yu's abode.

In this elite academic environment, where Ms Yu studied for 10 consecutive years, Ms. Yu was not just another student; she was a young woman on the brink of discovering her potential, her aspirations nurtured within a community of like-minded peers. The school's legacy of empowering women resonated with Ms. Yu, instilling in her a sense of purpose and ambition that would guide her through the challenges and triumphs of her subsequent journey.

Through the lens of her educational experiences, Ms. Yu's narrative is one of growth, resilience, and the relentless pursuit of excellence. Her story, interwoven with the influence of familial bonds and the guiding hands of mentors like Mrs. Lee, reflects the broader tapestry of life's complexities and the indelible impact of early decisions on one's future path.

Chapter 09:
For friendships made, and pleasures shared?

Within the prestigious corridors and manicured lawns of her elite school, Ms. Yu walked a path that was starkly different from those chauffeured in luxury. Each morning, as she boarded the school bus, a microcosm of society unfolded before her young eyes, a vivid tableau of the economic disparities that threaded through her life. This journey, though physically taxing, was spiritually enlightening, forging within her resilience and a perspective far beyond her years.

Her companions on these bus rides, fellow travelers on this early dawn journey, became her closest allies. Together, they shared not just a seat but a silent acknowledgment of their shared circumstances. These friendships, born of necessity and nurtured through countless mornings and afternoons, were her sanctuary, a counterbalance to the opulence that defined the school's social landscape.

As the bus wove its way through the city, making its diligent stops to gather its precious cargo, Ms. Yu's mind would wander to the lives of her wealthy schoolmates. She pondered their lives as they arrived in chauffeured Bentleys and Jaguars, the narratives spun within the walls of their grand homes. Yet, it was the understanding and camaraderie found in her bus companions that offered her the most comfort and inspiration. Often, she found her schoolmates who had chauffeurs were usually the most spoilt children whose experiences are far removed from reality. They were often snooty, and snobbish, kept to their cliques, had sleepovers amongst themselves, brought the nicest stationeries, had libraries of their own books, and played the latest handheld computer games. Their parents would throw parties where they only invited their own cliques, and they were the majority. Mrs. Yu thus felt trapped in middle class, with schoolmates from a very different social class.

The social stratification at school was a daily lesson, one not found in textbooks but in the lived experiences of its students. The hierarchy was unspoken yet palpable, a silent orchestra conducting the symphony of school life. Those who walked to school in the tropical heat, their paths shaded by the canopies of heritage trees, were the enigmatic figures in this social ballet. Their proximity to the school was a marker of status just as potent as the luxury cars that graced the driveway.

By the tender age of ten, Ms. Yu's worldview had crystallized into a firm resolve. She was determined not just to climb the social ladder but to leap over it, to carve a niche for herself where the distinctions of birth and wealth were mere footnotes to her achievements.

The stark disparities of her school days, rather than daunting her, served as the forge upon which her character was tempered. Ms. Yu's aspirations were not merely dreams but declarations of intent, a promise to herself and to the world that she would transcend the boundaries set before her. Her journey, marked by early mornings and introspective bus rides, was a testament to the power of resilience, ambition, and the enduring belief in one's own potential to effect change.

This educational odyssey, set against the backdrop of Singapore's meritocratic yet divided society, was a crucible for Ms. Yu. It taught her lessons of humility, perseverance, and the intrinsic value of forging deep, meaningful connections with those who shared her journey. As she navigated the complexities of adolescence against this multifaceted social backdrop, Ms. Yu wanted to be part of the elite class. She hungered for more, to be part of their world.

Chapter 10:
Threads of Color: Friendship, Diversity, and Growth

In her formative years, Ms. Yu's academic journey was interspersed with the vibrant hues of cherished friendships, painting her school days with broad strokes of joy, learning, and discovery. These relationships, particularly with Annie Khoo and her sole Indian friend, Priyanka; both of whom also studied in the same school, became the threads weaving the rich tapestry of her childhood, each strand imbued with its unique color and texture.

Annie Khoo, with her Peranakan heritage, was more than a friend; she was a mirror reflecting Ms. Yu's own ambitions and intellect. Their rivalry, particularly evident during Sunday school sessions, was not merely a contest but a dance of mutual admiration and respect. On Sundays after church, It was in the warmth of the Khoo household, amidst the laughter and challenges over computer games, that Ms. Yu found a second family. The Khoos, with their intellectual pursuits and eventual move to Australia, left an indelible mark on Ms. Yu, illustrating the profound impact of mentorship and intellectual camaraderie on young minds. This separation, though poignant, underscored the transient nature of childhood friendships, leaving Ms. Yu with a repository of memories and lessons that would guide her in her own journey. When Mrs Yu became a mother herself and struggled with Peter's language disorder; it was Annie's mother, Mrs Khoo who would be a beacon, pointing the way to the education psychologist who helped in Peter's diagnosis.

Conversely, her friendship with the Indian girl, Priyanka, a beacon of diversity in their predominantly Chinese milieu, offered Ms. Yu a window into the kaleidoscopic world of cultural richness and empathy. This relationship was a testament to the power of friendship to transcend racial diversity, fostering an environment of inclusivity and mutual respect. It was through this bond that Ms. Yu learned to appreciate the nuances of different cultures and understand the beauty of Singapore's multicultural tapestry. Singapore is the melting pot of 3 main races; Chinese, Malay, and Indian. Most Singaporeans are the descendants of people who immigrated from countries like China, India, Malaysia, and Indonesia.

These friendships, set against the backdrop of early school bus rides and shared experiences, were not merely incidental. They were instrumental in shaping Ms. Yu's worldview, teaching her the values of diversity, empathy, and the importance of forging deep, meaningful connections. They underscored the lessons imparted by her family, enriching her academic pursuits with the depth of real-world experiences and the understanding that success is not only measured by one's achievements but also by the richness of one's relationships and the breadth of one's empathy.

As Ms. Yu navigated through the years of compulsory education, these friendships became the cornerstone of her personal development, each interaction, and each shared moment contributing to the mosaic of her identity. They provided a counterbalance to the academic rigors and social hierarchies of school life, offering solace, inspiration, and a sense of belonging. Through these relationships, Ms. Yu learned to balance the pursuit of academic excellence with the cultivation of personal relationships, understanding that both were critical in carving out a successful and fulfilling life.

In the grand tapestry of Ms. Yu's life, these early friendships were vivid threads, each adding to the complexity and beauty of her story. They were reminders of the joy found in shared experiences, the growth spurred by intellectual challenges and the lasting impact of connections forged in the crucible of youth. As Ms. Yu looked back on these years, she saw not just the path she had traversed but also the people who had walked it with her, each leaving an indelible mark on her journey toward self-discovery and success.

Chapter 11:
Intellectual Foundations and Meritocratic Milestones

The journey through the formative years of Ms. Yu's education was marked not just by her academic prowess but also by the nuanced experiences that framed her understanding of the world. With a natural affinity for languages and humanities, she not only excelled in her studies but also developed a deep appreciation for the rich tapestry of human history and culture. This intellectual curiosity was both a beacon and a compass as she navigated through the complexities of her early education.

The culmination of the Primary School journey was the Primary School Leaving Examination (PSLE), a crucible that tested the mettle of every young Singaporean. For Ms. Yu, scoring 252 points was a significant achievement, placing her within the top 10% of her cohort. This moment was more than a personal victory; it was a reflection of how academically gifted she was as she had hardly put in any work for the PSLE exams.

In the competitive landscape of Singapore's educational system in the 1990s, the PSLE was not merely an assessment but a determinant of one's academic and, by extension, professional future. The score a child received acted as a gatekeeper, funneling students into tracks that would dictate the caliber of education they would receive henceforth. This system, predicated on the allocation of the best resources to the most academically gifted, underscored a meritocratic ethos that permeated Singaporean society.

The anxiety surrounding the PSLE, palpable among students and parents alike, stemmed from the widespread recognition of its pivotal role in shaping a child's future. The examination stood as a societal milestone, a sacred cow within the educational landscape, revered and unassailable. It was a reflection of a broader cultural ethos that valued academic achievement as a cornerstone of success and societal contribution.

For Ms. Yu, navigating this environment was a testament to her academic prowess. Her success in the PSLE was not just a reflection of her intellectual capabilities but also her ability to thrive within a system that demanded excellence and rewarded merit. But you know the saying, 'Pride always goes before a fall'.

Chapter 12:
Navigating Adolescence and Academic Trials

Reflecting on her adolescence, Ms. Yu confronted the uncomfortable truth of her past disdain for her own parents. Amidst a world where peers were chauffeured to school and parents boasted impressive education and wealth, Ms. Yu felt a misguided shame towards her own family's more modest means. This sentiment led her to discourage her parents from attending school events, fearing judgment based on their attire or mannerisms, which she perceived as less sophisticated compared to those of her friend's parents.

This period of introspection revealed a blend of adolescent arrogance and a lapse in her academic dedication, particularly after her early academic success placed her in the top 10% nationally. Joining the Girls' Brigade offered a new focus, immersing her in activities and competitions that, while enriching, drew her away from her studies and family life.

The distance this created at home led to a profound moment in Ms. Yu's life when, at 14, she learned of her mother's pregnancy. The arrival of a new sibling at a crucial juncture in her academic journey brought unexpected distractions and the family stopped attending church on Sundays as Mrs Chan felt that it was too much of a hassle to bring a baby/ toddler to church.

As Ms. Yu stepped into the complex world of high school, she was met with academic challenges that tested her resolve and shaped her future path. Encountering subjects like Physics and Additional Math presented significant hurdles, and the educational system's rigorous streaming process deemed her unfit for subjects like Biology and eventually Additional Math, further narrowing her academic and career options. The teachers persuaded her not to take Biology and Additional Math simply because they did not want Mrs Yu's grades to affect the school's ranking in these subjects. In the face of these setbacks, Ms. Yu was a bit miffed by the school and their priorities. She felt that her interests were not considered. Nonetheless, The decision to drop Biology and Higher Math under pressure from her school to maintain its academic standing was a pivotal moment, redirecting her focus toward the humanities, where her true passions lay.

Her Math teacher was most direct, "Your Additional Math and Biology results are not very good. Can you please drop those subjects so that you do not affect the subject ranking in our school?"

There were also teachers who did not mince words and were particularly harsh and cruel towards Mrs Yu. In an art lesson, she innocently asked her teacher,

"What color would I get if I mixed red and blue?"

The teacher snappily replied, "Are you blind? Mix it and see for yourself!"

That response turned Mrs. Yu off anything related to artistic production forever.

On another occasion, Mrs Yu's Chemistry teacher, "Change, will you?? I always tell you to improve, why can't you improve?? And lose some weight, will you?? You look like Lydia Sum!" (Lydia Sum was a very plump Hong Kong comedian)

Some rather unkind classmates would also say, "You don't walk properly! You seem to be perpetually bouncing on your feet! Haha! I shall call you Dancing Hippo!" And the moniker stuck for the rest of high school.

In the face of all this verbal bullying by teachers and classmates alike in a supposedly elite school, Mrs Yu did not do particularly well in the GCE O levels. She only managed As in English, Math, and Geography, and Bs in the rest. With that, she moved on to Junior College. By now, she was totally jaded by all the subjects she had taken in secondary school.

The only high point of Secondary school was the opportunity Ms Yu was given to be the commanding officer of a small squadron of girls in the Girls Brigade. The culmination of the season was in an Annual Drill Competition. She expertly led her squadron to a convincing victory on the very day of the competition. It took a whole year of gruelling commitment and the experience laid the foundation for leadership qualities in her later life.

Chapter 13:
From Adversity to Academia: The Junior College

Her journey through the educational system continued to be marked by a lot of regrets. The transition to Junior College brought with it the opportunity to explore new subjects such as Economics, History, Principles of Accounting, and Management of Business, diverging from the familiar path she had followed until then. However, this decision to embrace entirely new fields of study, while bold, came with its own set of challenges. The requirement to master Higher Math previously dropped, now loomed large, yet by this stage, Ms. Yu had grown in confidence and capability, tackling the subject with newfound vigor.

Transitioning into junior college marked a significant shift in Ms. Yu's educational journey, not just academically but socially as well. For the first time, after a decade in an all-girls environment, she found herself in a co-educational setting, introducing an entirely new dynamic to her school life. This change sparked a heightened self-awareness and a critical view of her physical appearance, leading her down a path of extreme dieting that would challenge her health and self-image for years to come.

The introduction of male classmates stirred a self-consciousness in Ms. Yu that she hadn't experienced before. In an attempt to conform to her own standards of beauty and acceptance, she embarked on a crash diet that was both drastic and dangerous, limiting her food intake to the bare minimum. This period of self-imposed starvation not only disrupted her physical health, leading to a cessation of her menstrual cycle but also culminated in a physical injury that brought her to a moment of isolation and reflection.

A seemingly innocent invitation to go ice skating resulted in a broken ankle, a consequence of her weakened state. This incident, and the subsequent lack of familial support during her hospital stay, forced Ms. Yu to confront her choices and the toll her body image struggles were taking on her life. Alone in the hospital, she turned to her faith, finding solace and a renewed sense of purpose in her relationship with God, a relationship she had neglected since the birth of her sister Carol.

This period of Ms. Yu's life was a testament to her evolving academic identity, marked by moments of self-discovery, perseverance, and the relentless pursuit of personal growth.

Despite these personal challenges, Ms. Yu persevered academically, despite the poor choice of attempting subjects she had never encountered before and taking the A-level exams within a year of preparation! This time, she only managed Bs and Cs. These grades were good enough for her admission to the National University of Singapore. There, she chose to study English Language and History, as Singapore was in the midst of the worldwide financial crisis (1997) at that point in time and Mrs Yu felt that a teaching career would be the most prudent choice for someone of her middle-class social status. She couldn't help but feel a deep sense of envy as her former schoolmates from secondary school and Junior College had parents who could pay for their university education in countries like the United States and the United Kingdom. This choice marked the beginning of a new chapter in her life, one where her past experiences would inform her future.

Chapter 14:
Redefining Success

For Mr. and Mrs. Chan, their daughter's acceptance into the university was a beacon of hope and a testament to their sacrifices. Lacking the opportunity for higher education themselves, they swelled with pride at Ms. Yu's accomplishment. Yet, beneath this family triumph, Ms. Yu harbored her own reservations. Her grades, though sufficient to secure her university placement, fell short of her aspirations for law school—a path she deemed more prestigious and fitting for her ambitions. This sense of unfulfilled potential was further accentuated by the success of a close friend from junior college, who not only entered Law School but also later married a classmate, who went on to become a Cabinet Minister, a union that seemed to epitomize both professional and personal achievement. This juxtaposition of paths, Ms. Yu's own and that of her friend, underscored a journey of introspection and self-discovery, challenging her to find contentment and pride in her own achievements while navigating the complexities of ambition and success.

Before embarking on her university journey, Mrs. Chan treated Ms. Yu to a shopping spree, a gesture of support and celebration for her daughter's new chapter. Adorned in smart dresses and pantsuits, Ms. Yu stepped into her freshman year with a sense of style but a subdued ambition. The dreams of climbing social ladders and achieving financial success had faded, replaced by more modest aspirations shaped by the reality of her chosen field of study and the economic climate of the 1997 financial crisis.

Ms. Yu's ambitions had evolved; she now aspired for a stable family life rather than professional accolades. This shift in priorities was reflected in her personal commitments as well. Following her hospitalization and a newfound dedication to her faith, she deepened her engagement with the community, volunteering at hospitals, and reaffirming her commitment to church alongside a childhood connection from her past, the youngest Lee sibling. This period of her life was marked by introspection, community service, and a reevaluation of what success meant to her, set against the backdrop of Singapore's challenging economic landscape.

In the tapestry of Ms. Yu's life, her relationship with her younger sister, Carol, added vibrant threads of joy, mischief, and occasional frustration. Carol, with her youthful exuberance, became both a source of delight and a challenge. Carol taught Ms. Yu lessons in patience, responsibility, and the nuances of sisterhood.

Ms Yu also started making her own keep via giving private tuition to secondary and primary school students. She stopped receiving an allowance from her parents when she turned 19 because she felt that she should be self sufficient. Her parents were already paying for her university education which was highly subsidized by the government.

As Ms. Yu navigated the new digital age at university, the internet opened doors to uncharted social landscapes. It was through these virtual corridors that she connected with a person who would profoundly impact her future. This meeting, facilitated by the burgeoning world of Internet Relay Chat, blossomed into a relationship that fulfilled Ms. Yu's aspirations for companionship, love, and stability. Her new partner, embodying qualities she admired, became an integral part of her journey, transforming her daily life and reinforcing the belief that the paths we tread can lead to unexpected, yet fulfilling destinations.

Chapter 15:
Navigating the Property Waves of 1980s and 1990s Singapore

This chapter is to depict what was happening in Singapore in the 1980s and 1990s when the time Mrs Yu was in primary and secondary school; highlighting the wealth disparity that was so apparent to her between herself and her schoolmates. The key to some of the wealth was the property market in Singapore. Just like in Hong Kong, where many millionaires are made; due to the property market.

In the bustling streets of 1980s and 90s Singapore, the property market emerged as a beacon of opportunity amidst economic turbulence. As the nation grappled with the aftermath of the 1986 oil crisis and navigated through the tumultuous waters of the 1997 global financial crisis, the property market stood as a bastion of stability and prosperity for many.

In the early 1990s, Singapore witnessed a residential property boom of unprecedented proportions. Fuelled by a confluence of factors, including economic stability, rising purchasing power, and government policies promoting home ownership, the property market soared to speculative heights. The allure of property investment was irresistible, as young Singaporeans were urged to marry, immigration policies were revised, and double-income households became the norm.

Against this backdrop, property emerged as the investment of choice, offering superior returns compared to other asset classes. With low-interest rates, property ownership became synonymous with wealth and prosperity. As a result, speculative buying became rampant, with stories of exorbitant profits fueling the frenzy.

Sub-sales, where properties were bought and sold even before completion, became the norm, leading to midnight queues and unprecedented demand for condominium launches. The market was driven by speculation, with prices skyrocketing to unsustainable levels.

The early 1990s were a period of economic optimism and growth for Singapore. After weathering the storm of the 1986 oil crisis, the nation's economy rebounded, driven by robust export growth and government-led initiatives to promote domestic demand. As incomes rose and consumer confidence soared, Singaporeans began to look towards property as a lucrative investment opportunity.

One of the key drivers of the property boom was the government's pro-homeownership policies. Since independence, the government has placed a strong emphasis on promoting homeownership as a means of building social stability and fostering a sense of national identity. Through schemes such as the Housing Development Board (HDB) flats and the Central Provident Fund (CPF), Singaporeans were encouraged to invest in property as a way of securing their financial future.

Today, the property market remains a key pillar of Singapore's economy, albeit one that is closely monitored and regulated to prevent a repeat of past mistakes. Singapore is regarded like a Switzerland of Asia; where the rich and wealthy from around the world make safe and sound investments and set up family offices for wealth management purposes. There is only one way property prices go in Singapore; in the long run, upwards! Property is a safe investment for capital gains. To add to its allure; the government does not impose capital gains tax!

Chapter 16:
From Cyberspace to Altar: A Millennium Love Story

The days that followed Ms. Yu's meeting with Mr. Yu were like something out of a fairytale. Love blossomed between them, and Ms. Yu found herself showered with affection and adoration. Mr. Yu, several years her senior and financially stable, treated her like royalty. Despite not being particularly religious, he willingly accompanied Ms. Yu to church, eager to be part of her world.

Their love story was unconventional, born from the depths of cyberspace at a time when online relationships were still met with skepticism. Yet, against all odds, their connection proved to be genuine and enduring. By the turn of the millennium, they were already discussing marriage, setting a date for December 2000. Ms. Yu was overjoyed at the prospect of becoming a millennium bride, and preparations for the grand celebration were set in motion.

The wedding festivities spanned two extravagant days, with a lavish lunch at the Conrad International Hotel followed by a sumptuous dinner at the Mandarin Hotel. Surrounded by more than 50 tables of guests, the newlyweds basked in the glow of their love and the warmth of their loved ones' blessings. At just 22 years old, Ms. Yu stepped into her new role as Mrs. Yu, ready to embark on the journey of marriage.

Mr. Yu hailed from a humble background, with parents who lacked formal education but were dedicated civil servants. Despite their modest means, they welcomed Ms. Yu into their family with open arms, even going so far as to secure a million-dollar property in their name as a gesture of their affection and acceptance. Though the property belonged to Mr. Yu and his parents, the couple received a spacious five-bedroom home to start their married life together. From living in a lofty middle-class flat 17 stories in the sky, Mrs Yu now lived in a highly coveted landed property; the pinnacle of every Singaporean's dream.

For Ms. Yu, the move couldn't come soon enough. Living under the same roof as her grandfather had become unbearable, his disapproval weighing heavily on her aspirations. Despite her grandfather's lofty expectations for her, all Ms. Yu desired now was a simple life with a loving husband and three children before the age of 30. The toxic environment of her childhood home, tainted by her grandfather's heavy smoking and repeated taunts that she had let down the Chan family due to her failure to get into law school, only fueled her desire to break free and forge her own path.

Amidst the excitement of her impending marriage, Ms. Yu received an unexpected opportunity to pursue an Honours year in History, delaying her graduation from university until after her wedding. Despite the added pressure, she embraced the challenge, determined to further her education and secure a brighter future for herself.

After the lavish wedding ceremony, approximately 6 months later, Mrs Yu's graduated from university. Almost about the same time, both Grandpa and Grandma Chan passed from this life within months of each other, leaving behind a legacy that would shape her future. With astute financial planning, Mr. and Mrs. Chan turned their inheritance of that lofty flat in the sky into investments, making the deposit for 3 private properties that would provide stability and security for years to come. At just 23 years old, Ms. Yu found herself navigating the complexities of homeownership and investment, as her teaching salary allowed her to get a mortgage for one of the 3 private properties the astute Mrs Chan invested in, laying the foundation for a prosperous future ahead. Mr and Mrs Chan and their daughter Carol lived in one, and the other two were tenanted. The tenants pay the mortgage while the property appreciates in capital year on year.

Chapter 17:
Against the Current

In the heart of bustling Singapore, amidst the towering skyscrapers and bustling streets, Ms. Yu found herself at a crossroads in her career. Armed with a passion for education and a desire to make a difference, she embarked on a journey as a teacher, eager to mold young minds and shape the future generation.

But as she soon discovered, the path of a teacher was not always smooth sailing. Ms. Yu quickly realized that she was not cut out for the traditional mold of a team player in the workplace. She had her own ideas, her own methods, and a fierce independence that often rubbed her colleagues and superiors the wrong way.

Her altruistic ambitions for her students drove her to push boundaries and challenge norms, but in doing so, she inadvertently ruffled feathers and alienated herself from those around her. Despite her best intentions, she found herself labeled as a maverick, unable to find her footing in any school for more than a couple of years.

It was a pattern that repeated itself time and time again as she moved from one school to another, seeking a place where she could truly make a difference. Each new environment brought its own set of challenges and triumphs, shaping Ms. Yu's understanding of education and her role within it.

And then, in 2006, fate led her to a prestigious secondary school nestled among the city's elite. This was no ordinary school; it was a beacon of excellence, attracting the brightest minds and the most affluent families in Singapore. Ms. Yu found herself teaching the sons of presidents and principals, surrounded by the cream of the crop in the teaching world.

But beneath the veneer of privilege and intellect, she saw something else – a hidden darkness lurking beneath the surface. Many of her students seemed to be grappling with inner demons, struggling to find their place in the world despite their outward success.

Driven by compassion and a desire to help, Ms. Yu embarked on a journey of her own, enrolling in a master's program in counseling psychology. She wanted to understand the complexities of the teenage mind and provide support to those who needed it most.

As she delved deeper into her studies, Ms. Yu became increasingly aware of the importance of mental health in education. She saw firsthand the toll that academic pressure and societal expectations could take on young minds, and she was determined to make a difference.

For her, teaching was not just about imparting knowledge; it was about nurturing the holistic development of each and every student under her care.

She believed passionately in the power of counseling and therapy, not just for students, but for teachers as well, especially young teachers.

In her eyes, education was not just about academics; it was about fostering emotional intelligence, resilience, and empathy. And so, armed with her newfound knowledge and empathy, Ms. Yu set out to change the world, one student at a time, one counseling session at a time.

Despite the challenges she faced along the way, Ms. Yu remained steadfast in her belief that every child deserved the chance to thrive – academically, emotionally, and socially. And as she continued on her journey, she knew that she was making a difference, one small step at a time.

Chapter 18:
Embracing New Frontiers in Counseling and Motherhood

In the midst of the hustle and bustle of 2007, Ms. Yu found herself at a crossroads in her career. Despite her passion for teaching, she yearned for a new challenge, a chance to make a difference in a different way. Armed with a fresh master's degree in counseling, she took a leap of faith and embarked on a journey into the world of professional counseling.

Her first foray into this new field led her to the Ministry of Defense, where she was tasked with providing support and guidance to the young men who faced compulsory conscription. It was a daunting responsibility, but one that Ms. Yu embraced wholeheartedly.

As she settled into her new role, fate intervened in the form of a new addition to her family. Just as she was finding her footing as a counselor, Ms. Yu discovered that she was pregnant with her first child, Peter. It was a joyous moment, tinged with the uncertainty of balancing motherhood with her newfound career.

One of the unique challenges of being a counselor in the military was the requirement to be on call overnight, ready to lend a listening ear to distressed service personnel in their darkest moments. However, due to her pregnancy, Ms. Yu was exempted from this duty, much to the chagrin of her colleagues.

Despite the initial skepticism from some of her peers, Ms. Yu was fortunate to have a compassionate and understanding leader at the helm of the counseling unit. Under his guidance, she was able to navigate the delicate balance between her professional responsibilities and the demands of impending motherhood.

With his unwavering support, Ms. Yu was able to embrace her role as a counselor with renewed determination and dedication. She poured her heart and soul into her work, providing a beacon of hope for those in need, both within the military and beyond.

Life as a counselor in the Ministry of Defense was a journey into a world filled with both challenges and rewards. From the viewpoint of a casual observer, it may have seemed idyllic, with its structured tea and lunch breaks and Ms. Yu's spacious office where she conducted her counseling sessions. But behind the veneer of routine lay a complex tapestry of human emotions and struggles.

Ms. Yu's days were a whirlwind of activity, filled to the brim with young men between the ages of 17 and 21, all grappling with the realities of military conscription. In Singapore, mandatory military service is a rite of passage for all male citizens, a two-year commitment that often comes as a shock to those accustomed to the freedoms of civilian life.

From the moment her first client walked through the door at 8:30 a.m., Ms. Yu found herself immersed in a world of uncertainty and vulnerability. Many of her clients struggled to adapt to the strict regimentation of military life, yearning for the freedoms they once took for granted. They sought solace in her office, hoping for a moment of respite from the harsh realities of their barracks.

But amidst the sea of familiar struggles, there were also those whose battles were far more profound. Ms. Yu encountered young men grappling with undiagnosed mental illnesses, their minds plagued by hallucinations and delusions. Some even expressed violent intentions, threatening harm to their superiors and comrades alike.

In those moments, Ms. Yu's role transcended that of a mere counselor. She became a lifeline, navigating the delicate balance between compassion and caution. With each case, she walked a tightrope, ensuring that her clients received the care and support they desperately needed while safeguarding the safety of those around them.

For some, the journey ended with a premature discharge from military service, a bittersweet reprieve from the burdens of duty. Yet, for others, the road ahead remained fraught with uncertainty, their struggles with mental illness casting a long shadow over their futures.

Reflecting on her experiences, Ms. Yu couldn't help but recognize the critical role that mandatory conscription played in identifying and addressing mental health issues within Singaporean society. In a country where rapid development had outpaced the growth of mental health services, the military served as a vital checkpoint, ensuring that those in need received the attention they deserved.

But beneath the surface lay a sobering truth – that the sacrifices of a few often served as a stark reminder of the broader societal challenges that lay ahead. As Singapore continued its journey of growth and transformation, Ms. Yu couldn't help but wonder if the mental health of its citizens would remain an overlooked casualty in the pursuit of progress.

In a world where reserves were measured in dollars and cents, she knew that it was time to redefine what it meant to truly prosper – not just in wealth, but in the well-being of every individual who called Singapore home. As she looked to the future, Ms. Yu vowed to continue her fight, one counseling session at a time, to ensure that no one would ever be left behind.

As she embarked on this new chapter of her life, Ms. Yu was reminded of the power of compassion, and understanding, and the importance of maintaining a healthy work-life balance. It was a lesson that would serve her well in the years to come, as she continued to touch the lives of those around her with her unwavering dedication and compassion.

Chapter 19:
Motherhood

As Ms. Yu entered her thirties, life took on a new dimension with the arrival of her first child, Peter. It was a momentous occasion, filled with joy and anticipation. She had thought she would have 3 children by the age of 30, but she managed to have only Peter.

With the birth of Peter, Ms. Yu found herself struggling to juggle the demands of motherhood and her career. Faced with the overwhelming task of raising a child, she made the difficult decision to seek refuge with her parents, the Chans. It was a move born out of necessity, as she knew she couldn't navigate this new chapter of her life without the support of her parents and helpers from Philippines.

One could hardly blame Mrs Yu, for she had grown up with helpers from the time she was born. She never learnt how to cook, clean nor wash as she was never expected to. Her childhood was spent with books. Her nose was always in her books; whether study or story books. Despite not growing up in wealth, she nonetheless never really ever had to lift a finger around the house. But now she had a baby!

Moving back in with her parents meant relying on their support and guidance to navigate the uncharted waters of motherhood. The Chans, ever supportive, welcomed their daughter, son in law and grandson with open arms, offering a safe haven amidst the chaos of everyday life. Mr and Mrs Yu purchased a bigger property for all of them to live in.

But even with the help of her family, the challenges of motherhood weighed heavily on Ms. Yu's shoulders. Juggling the demands of work and childcare proved to be a daunting task, made thankfully easier by the presence of a Filipino live-in helper tasked with assisting in Peter's care.

Despite the support she received, Ms. Yu couldn't shake the nagging sense of guilt that accompanied her daily routine. As she headed off to work each day, her mind would wander to thoughts of Peter, wondering if he was in good hands, if he was happy and well cared for. The Filipino helper she had at that point in time was not particularly reliable. She tried to earn extra income by cleaning other people's houses , despite being paid a good salary by the Chans and the Yus.

Eventually, the Yus decided to add one more Filipino helper to the family. They did it in good time, as the first one started stealing from them right under their noses! Nonetheless, the Chans and Yu knew the family couldn't function without their Filipino helpers and chose to forgive the first helper when she apologised for her actions.

Chapter 20:
Crossroads of Change

As fate would have it, Ms. Yu soon found herself at a crossroads in her career. Despite her initial enthusiasm for her role as a counselor in the military, she began to feel restless. The monotony of her daily routine left her yearning for something more, something that would ignite her passion and challenge her intellect.

In a moment of introspection, Ms. Yu began to question her own motivations and behaviors. Was it simply boredom that drove her to seek change, or was there something deeper at play? In a bold move, she turned the lens of scrutiny inward, embarking on a journey of self-discovery that would ultimately change the course of her life.

It was during this period of introspection that Ms. Yu stumbled upon a revelation: she believed she may be grappling with adult ADHD. The realization struck her like a bolt of lightning, illuminating the shadows of her mind with newfound clarity. Suddenly, her penchant for boredom and restlessness began to make sense, as did her insatiable thirst for novelty and excitement.

Armed with this newfound self-awareness, Ms. Yu made the daring decision to shake up her life once more. With a renewed sense of purpose and determination, she set her sights on greener pastures, determined to find fulfillment in a new environment.

And so, with unwavering resolve, Ms. Yu took a leap of faith and applied for a position as a counselor at a prestigious university. Her confidence was palpable as she breezed through the interview process, impressing her prospective employers with her intellect, empathy, and unwavering dedication to her craft.

But little did she know that this seemingly innocuous decision would set into motion a chain of events that would alter the trajectory of her life. With a sense of anticipation tinged with excitement, Ms. Yu bid farewell to her colleagues at the Ministry of Defence, ready to embrace the next chapter of her journey with open arms.

However, as she would soon discover, the path ahead was fraught with unforeseen challenges and pitfalls. What began as a simple desire for change would soon spiral into a maelstrom of chaos and uncertainty, testing Ms. Yu's resilience and determination in ways she never thought possible.

But amidst the turmoil and upheaval, one thing remained constant: Ms. Yu's unwavering belief in God and her ability to weather any storm that came her way. And so, with courage in her heart and fire in her soul, she embarked on a journey into the unknown, ready to confront whatever obstacles lay ahead with unwavering resolve and determination.

Chapter 21:
Betrayal in the Halls of Learning

In the corridors of academia, where dreams of higher education intertwine with the harsh realities of office politics, Ms. Yu found herself caught in a tangled web of ambition and betrayal.

Fresh from acing her interview for a coveted position on the university counseling team, Ms. Yu stepped into her new role with enthusiasm and determination. Little did she know, however, that she had already attracted the ire of her immediate superior, Jackie, before even setting foot in the office.

Unbeknownst to her, Jackie harbored reservations about welcoming Ms. Yu into the fold. But despite Jackie's reservations, her superior saw potential in Ms. Yu's background as a seasoned teacher and believed she would bring valuable insights to the counseling team.

The team itself was small, a tight-knit group tasked with guiding students through the maze of academic and personal challenges they faced. Eager to make her mark, Ms. Yu poured her heart and soul into her work, brimming with fresh ideas and a genuine desire to make a difference.

However, fate had other plans in store for Ms. Yu. Just as she was settling into her new role, she received the news that she was expecting her second child, Clara. Mrs Yu was shocked. She thought she had taken precautions against another pregnancy. She was still traumatised from the birth of Peter, who had to be delivered by Emergency Caesarean Section. She had no desire to go through pregnancy and childbirth again so soon after Peter.

Little did she know that Jackie would seize upon her pregnancy as an opportunity to sabotage her career. Jackie wasted no time in exploiting the situation to her advantage, painting Ms. Yu as an unreliable liability who would burden the team with her absence during maternity leave. With a few carefully chosen words, Jackie sowed seeds of doubt in the minds of her superiors, casting aspersions on Ms. Yu's commitment and suitability for the role.

Before she knew it, Ms. Yu found herself blindsided by a sudden ultimatum – she was to be let go from her position, her dreams of making a difference shattered by the cold machinations of office politics. It was a cruel twist of fate, a betrayal that cut deep into the core of her being.

Amidst the turmoil and heartache in addition to her disbelief about her new pregnancy, Mrs Yu plunged into deep depression. And though her journey had taken an unexpected turn, she refused to let the darkness dim the light of hope that burned within her heart. She knew that God would help her rise above adversity and forge a path toward a brighter tomorrow.

Chapter 22:
Embracing the Unexpected

In the wake of her unexpected pregnancy, Ms. Yu found herself plunged into a deep and overwhelming depression. The news of Clara's impending arrival came as a shock, catching her off guard and leaving her grappling with a whirlwind of emotions. It was a pregnancy she had not planned for, a curveball thrown into the carefully laid plans of her life.

As she struggled to come to terms with this new reality, Ms. Yu couldn't help but feel a sense of despair creeping in. The memories of Peter's traumatic birth still haunted her, casting a shadow over her impending delivery. The thought of another Emergency C-section filled her with dread, knowing all too well the pain of the recovery process that lay ahead.

But amidst the turmoil, a fire ignited within Ms. Yu—a fierce determination to fight for her rights and ensure a better future for herself and her growing family. She refused to let her pregnancy become a barrier to her career aspirations, refusing to accept anything less than her rightful entitlement to maternity benefits.

With steely resolve, Ms. Yu took on the university's HR department, challenging their discriminatory practices and threatening to escalate the issue to the Ministry of Manpower. She demanded nothing less than full recognition of her rights as a pregnant employee, refusing to back down until justice was served.

Her tenacity paid off, and the university, faced with the prospect of legal repercussions, capitulated to her demands. They agreed to grant her the maternity benefits she was entitled to, acknowledging the injustice of their initial stance. Yet, despite this small victory, the situation remained fraught with uncertainty.

Armed with nothing but her courage and resilience, Ms. Yu embarked on a job hunt unlike any other. She attended interviews, her burgeoning belly a visible testament to her impending motherhood. Yet, far from being deterred, she faced each challenge head-on, refusing to let her pregnancy define her or limit her prospects.

As fate would have it, just as Ms. Yu was on the cusp of embracing motherhood with the impending arrival of her daughter Clara, God decided to shower her with unexpected blessings. In a twist of serendipity, not one, but two job offers landed in her lap, offering her a chance to redefine her path.

The first offer came from the Prison Service, beckoning her to serve as a counselor for the incarcerated souls behind bars. It was a daunting yet noble calling, one that spoke to Ms. Yu's compassionate nature and her unwavering belief in the power of redemption.

The second offer, equally enticing, presented her with the opportunity to become a teacher for students hailing from the most disadvantaged backgrounds. It was a chance to make a real difference in the lives of those who needed it most, to be a guiding light in the darkness of their circumstances.

Having recently found herself at the receiving end of injustice, and unfair circumstance, the two different jobs interested her tremendously. She was sure no one set out in life wanting to be a criminal. No child deserves to be labelled a failure.

Ms. Yu found herself at a crossroads, torn between two paths that held the promise of fulfillment and purpose. But rather than choosing between them, she made a bold decision—to say yes to both.

With their start dates staggered months apart, Ms. Yu saw an opportunity to seize the moment, to embrace the challenge of juggling a newborn baby and not one, but two demanding jobs. It was a leap of faith, a leap into the unknown, but she was determined to make it work.

The memory of her past struggles, of being laid off and deemed unworthy, fueled her determination to succeed. She refused to let anyone dictate her worth or determine her fate. From that moment on, she vowed to give her all to every job that came her way, to prove her detractors wrong and carve out a future on her own terms.

With Clara nestled in her arms and a newfound sense of purpose coursing through her veins, Ms. Yu embarked on the journey ahead with a steely resolve and an unwavering belief in herself. For she knew that no obstacle was too great, no challenge too daunting, as long as she held fast to her dreams and never lost sight of the strength that lay within.

Chapter 23:
Navigating Motherhood and Career Ambitions

On the day America celebrated its independence, the world welcomed a new addition to the Yu family. Clara, with her rosy cheeks and sparkling eyes, brought boundless joy and love into their lives. For Ms. Yu, the journey of motherhood began anew, filled with tender moments and sleepless nights.

As the weeks passed, Ms. Yu felt a stirring within her, a desire to return to the workforce and reclaim a sense of purpose beyond the confines of home. Despite still receiving full maternity benefits from the university, she was determined to chart her own path. And so, in mid-September, barely two months after Clara's birth, she made the bold decision to start her commitment to the prison service.

Stepping into her new workplace, Ms. Yu found herself surrounded by a sea of men, much like her days in the military. Undeterred by the male-dominated environment, she dove headfirst into her role, eager to make a difference in the lives of those under her care.

With her home located a 45-minute drive away from Changi Prison, Ms. Yu enlisted the help of a second Filipino helper, Jennifer, to assist with the household chores and caring for little Clara. Juggling the demands of motherhood and a demanding job, she found herself constantly on the move, breastfeeding in the dead of night and rushing out the door at the crack of dawn.

But amidst the chaos of her dual roles, an accident struck one day. In her exhausted state, Ms. Yu accidentally collided her car with a pole while attempting to park, a stark reminder of the toll her busy schedule was taking on her well-being.

As she reflected on the incident, Ms. Yu realized that something had to give. With a heavy heart, she realized that she had to rest before she started her teaching job, so she tendered her resignation from the prison service. She had spent barely 2 months on the job.

In January, as the new school year dawned, she started the second job that she had committed to before giving birth to Clara, promising a higher salary and greater stability for her growing family.

Pragmatic and forward-thinking, Ms. Yu weighed her options carefully. With two mouths to feed and bills to pay, she knew that she had to choose the path that would secure their future. And so, with a sense of determination and resolve, she bid farewell to one small chapter of her life and embraced the next with open arms.

Chapter 24:
Unlocking Potential Against the Odds

Three and a half years had passed since Mrs Yu bid farewell to the teaching profession, never imagining she would return. Back in 2007, she had thought her days of shaping young minds were over for good. Yet, as the dawn of 2011 approached, she found herself stepping back into the classroom once more.

Her recent years spent counseling and working with the less privileged in Singapore have equipped her with a unique perspective. Now, she was the perfect candidate to work with the children of Singapore's lowest social hierarchy. These were the students who had fallen through the cracks, failed by a system that seemed stacked against them from the start.

Most of Mrs Yu's new students had stumbled at the hurdle of the PSLE, their academic futures seemingly doomed before they even began. Their parents, often struggling with their own challenges, lacked the time, education, or resources to support their children's learning. Private lessons were a luxury beyond their reach, leaving these students to fend for themselves in a system that offered little room for second chances.

But Mrs Yu saw potential where others saw failure. She recognized that these students, often overlooked and underestimated, possessed unique talents and abilities waiting to be unlocked. It was a fresh approach to education, one that appealed to her altruistic spirit and ignited a passion within her to make a difference.

Her role as an English teacher was just the beginning. Soon, she found herself wearing many hats – counselor, advocate, and sometimes even surrogate parent. She made house visits to understand why her students were absent, uncovering heartbreaking stories of hardship and resilience.

Working closely with the school's counselors, Mrs Yu tackled the deep-rooted issues facing her students and their families. It was an uphill battle, but one she was determined to fight, armed with compassion and a relentless belief in her students' potential.

Unlike conventional secondary schools, where resources were stretched thin, Mrs Yu's new workplace prioritized support for its most vulnerable students. With one counselor dedicated to each secondary level, the school was a beacon of hope in a sea of adversity.

It was a vision championed by the school's first principal, a trailblazer with a heart of gold. Supported by the Minister of Education, who would later become the

President of Singapore, the school received ample funding to provide for its students' needs.

One such initiative was the provision of free meals, a simple yet powerful gesture that encouraged students to attend school and nourished their bodies and minds. But Mrs Yu's dedication went beyond the classroom walls. She sought to broaden her students' horizons, organizing trips to museums, art galleries, and other attractions around Singapore.

With funding from the school, she made sure her students had the opportunity to experience the rich cultural tapestry of their city-state, instilling in them a sense of wonder and possibility. It was her way of showing them that education was not just about textbooks and exams but about exploring the world around them and discovering their place within it.

And so, armed with determination and a boundless love for her students, Mrs Yu embarked on a journey to uplift and empower those whom society had overlooked. In her classroom, every day was a chance to rewrite the narrative and pave the way for a brighter future, one filled with hope, opportunity, and endless possibilities.

Chapter 25:
Embracing Dual Roles and New Beginnings

Even as she dedicated herself to her teaching career, her heart longed for something more. She yearned to delve deeper into the world of counseling, to explore new avenues of healing and growth. And so, in the midst of her tenure at the school, she embarked on a journey to further her qualifications. She started on a postgraduate diploma in Supervising Counsellors.

Amidst the hustle and bustle of daily life, Ms. Yu found herself juggling two very different roles. By day, she was a dedicated teacher, guiding her students through the intricacies of academia. But as the sun dipped below the horizon, she transformed into something else entirely—a beacon of hope and guidance for aspiring counselors.

Her skills in counseling were unparalleled, honed over years of experience and a genuine desire to help others navigate life's challenges. Ms. Yu was always there, ready to lend a listening ear and a comforting word. She applied these same skills to aspiring counselors as she became a supervisor to many.

Having been teased mercilessly as a student and unfairly managed as an employee, Mrs Yu was the most empathetic teacher, counsellor and counselling supervisor. She knew exactly how it felt like to be slighted, to be made to feel unworthy, to be made to feel like less than nothing.

Ms. Yu's dedication to her students and their families knew no bounds, and she remained steadfast in her role until mid-2013. It was the longest she had ever stayed in one workplace, a testament to her unwavering commitment and passion for her craft.

With determination and perseverance, within a year, Ms. Yu achieved a Diploma in Supervision, granting her the authority to oversee and guide other counselors in their practice. It was a milestone she cherished, a validation of her expertise and dedication to her craft.

As she navigated the complexities of her dual roles, Ms. Yu found solace in her new home in District 10, where she now resided with her husband, Mr. Yu, their two children, and their Filipino helper. She had moved out of her family home as the children were older now and needed more space. But despite the comfort of her surroundings, she couldn't help but start to feel restless again. It was in her DNA, this constant need for change. She tried to quell it, for she still remembered what happened the last time she craved change.

Little did she know, the winds of change were indeed about to sweep through her life, altering its course in ways she never could have imagined. Though she didn't pray nor ask for it, fate had a way of intervening, steering her toward a destiny she didn't dream of. God had big plans for her, but he was not letting on just what it was just yet.

Chapter 26:
Paving the Path to Purpose and Prosperity

In the tapestry of Ms. Yu's life, the year 2013 emerged as a pivotal chapter, one that would alter the course of her journey in ways she could never have imagined. At the time, she found herself balancing the responsibilities of her part-time role as a supervisor of counselors while navigating the intricate webs of government procurement.

It was during this period that Ms. Yu stumbled upon a government website dedicated to procurement opportunities. The counseling school where she occasionally lent her expertise sought her assistance in submitting proposals for projects initiated by the Singaporean government. Among the myriad calls for bids, one particular project caught her eye—a noble endeavor spearheaded by the Prison Department of the Ministry of Home Affairs.

The project aimed to facilitate the reintegration of short-sentence convicts, convicted of petty crimes, back into society while mitigating the risk of recidivism. Intrigued by the prospect of making a meaningful impact, Ms. Yu found herself impulsively responding to the call for bids, despite lacking a company or a team of counselors to support her endeavor.

With a sense of curiosity and a dash of audacity, she navigated through the online procurement system, treating the bidding process as a mere experiment. Little did she know that her impromptu bid would soon catapult her into uncharted territory.

Weeks passed, and Ms. Yu found herself engulfed in the routine of her day-to-day life. But fate had other plans in store for her. One fateful day, as she went about her duties at the school, the shrill ring of her phone shattered the monotony of her surroundings.

Answering the call, she was greeted by a familiar voice—a representative from the Prison Department, her former employer from years past. A wave of confusion washed over her as she struggled to comprehend the reason for their unexpected call.

"Am I speaking to Mrs Yu?" the voice inquired.

"Yes, I am," replied Ms. Yu, her voice tinged with uncertainty.

"I'm calling to congratulate you on your successful bid for the project with the Prison Department," the voice continued.

"What?" gasped Ms. Yu, her mind reeling with disbelief.

"Yes, you are the ONLY bidder. We know you from the past. We trust you can do the job," the voice explained, a note of assurance evident in their tone.

And just like that, God opened the way for Ms. Yu to leave her teaching job and start on her new life as an entrepreneur. In a twist of fate, she was handed a huge six-figure sum, a seed of opportunity that would start her on a fast track journey to millionaire status.

Ms. Yu made the snap decision to leave her teaching job. As she bid farewell to the classroom, she embraced a new calling with fervor and determination.

Determined to make a difference, Ms. Yu embarked on a journey to support ex-offenders in their quest for redemption. With a tender heart and a keen sense of purpose, she assembled a team of dedicated counselors, each sharing her passion for rehabilitation and second chances.

Together, they set up a counselling center in District 10, offering a safe haven for those seeking guidance and support. Ms. Yu quickly realized that one of the key factors to mitigating recidivism was to provide ex offenders with a job! Singapore is a city that had an extremely high cost of living and everyone wants to keep up with the Jones! It is an extremely stressful enviroment to live in and there are many temptations to break the law in the quest of making more money or saving money, saving time. From taking bribes in white collar crime, cheating on a parking ticket, jaywalking and consuming chewing gum, it is extremely easy to break the law in Singapore and be chastised for it. It doesn't help that there are security cameras everywhere and it is extremely easy to get caught. Drug consumption is also a crime.

Finding employment for her clients was no easy feat! In a society rife with stigma and prejudice, she became their unwavering advocate, tirelessly lobbying employers to give them a chance at a fresh start.

Yet, she soon discovered that the challenges facing ex-offenders went beyond mere employment. Many struggled with undiagnosed mental health issues, exacerbating their chances of reoffending. Determined to address this overlooked issue, Ms. Yu set out to provide holistic support, advocating for access to mental health services and counseling for all.

It was during one of her advocacy efforts that a passing comment sparked a revolutionary idea. What if she set up her own employment agency? Taking the suggestion to heart, Ms. Yu dove headfirst into the world of human resources, navigating the complexities of licensing and accreditation with tenacity and grace.

With her employment agency up and running, Ms. Yu's impact only grew stronger. Drawing on her extensive network and boundless determination, she not only secured jobs for her clients who were ex-offenders but also facilitated the recruitment of foreign labor from various parts of Asia for her corporate partners. Her already busy schedule soon saw her jetting off around the region in search of manpower. She made trips to Korea, China, Japan, and India to discuss recruitment options with business partners around Asia and was a beacon of light and hope for countless numbers of souls who were trying to find employment in prosperous Singapore to feed their families back home.

But Ms. Yu's ambitions didn't stop there. Empowered by her newfound role as a business owner, she expanded her counseling services to cater to government and private enterprises, offering vital support for employees' mental well-being. As she supervised her staff counselors, she gleaned so many interesting anecdotes of mental illness and disorders that she wrote a book chronicling the various types of mental disorders for the layman to read. She was fully committed to the idea that the men on the street should have basic knowledge of mental disorders so that they can provide mental health first aid to each other. She commissioned the printing of 1000 copies of her book, gave a good number of copies to the National Library in Singapore and the proceeds from the sale of the rest of the copies went fully to benefiting mental health charitable organizations in Singapore.

Her efforts did not go unnoticed. From Government agencies to private multinational corporations, Ms. Yu's company's services were in high demand, solidifying her reputation as a respected figure in both business and social circles. She was often quoted in various local print and radio media for her thoughts on mental health and mental illness and was a keen advocate and champion of sustainable employment for those who live with mental disorders.

At the zenith of her career, Mrs Yu was also approached by the People's Action Party, (the only political party to have control of Singapore since 1965) to have tea with a Minister alongside many other outstanding young people of her age. They hold such tea sessions to attract persons of calibre to their ranks. Needless to say, Mrs Yu kindly declined the offer to have tea. She was already part of the world she had only dreamt of. The world of the wealthy elite. She never harboured political ambitions of any kind.

Chapter 27:
Brushes with Royalty and Elite

As her success soared, so did her lifestyle. From luxury cars to designer wardrobes, Ms. Yu embraced the trappings of her newfound wealth with gusto, indulging her family in extravagant vacations and lavish experiences around the globe.

From the enchanting streets of Paris to the waterfalls in Norway, every destination was a testament to Ms. Yu's hard work and determination.

One particular comical vignette from this time took place on a Business Class Qatar Airways flight from Qatar to Stockholm. Surrounded by men in impeccably tailored military uniforms, Ms. Yu couldn't help but feel a sense of curiosity. However, she dismissed it as nothing out of the ordinary for a business class flight originating from the Middle East.

As the plane touched down in Stockholm, their excitement bubbled over, with Peter and Clara, aged only 7 and 9, eager to explore their new surroundings. However, in his youthful enthusiasm, Peter let loose a thunderous sneeze, unwittingly drawing the attention of one of the uniformed men.

To their astonishment, the man revealed himself to be none other than a member of the Swedish King Carl XVI Gustaf's entourage, politely requesting that they allow His Majesty to disembark first. The Yu family's jaws practically hit the floor as they realized they had been sharing a cabin with the King of Sweden all along, completely unaware of his presence.

It was a moment of sheer disbelief and embarrassment, as Peter's innocent sneeze at royalty turned into a comical mishap that they would never forget. But little did they know, this would not be their only encounter with the elite.

On another occasion, Ms. Yu found herself aboard a Singapore Airlines flight, this time in the prestigious First Class Suites cabin alongside the wife of the current Prime Minister of Singapore, Madam Ho Ching. Despite drawing the divider shut, Ms. Yu couldn't resist stealing glances at the powerful woman seated just a few feet away.

Madam Ho Ching exuded an aura of authority, her mere presence commanding respect from those around her. Throughout the flight, Ms. Yu observed as people approached Madam Ho Ching, eager to network and engage in business discussions even at 30,000 feet in the air.

After 4 years of very hard work and dedication, Mrs Yu made the decision to retire in 2017 to focus on her family, particularly her son Peter, who was grappling with a language disorder. By this time, before Mrs Yu turned 40, she was already a millionaire. Her assets exceeded her liabilities after tax by a Million USD. However, the punishing work schedule of an entrepreneur meant she had little time for her children. She had left the main task of child-rearing to her most trustworthy Filipino helper, Jennifer but she was often wrecked with guilt at the thought that she was not fulfilling her duties as a mother. She was well aware that children grew up in the twinkling of an eye, in a blink! Peter and Clara were such beautiful children. She didn't want to miss their childhood any longer.

Ms. Yu remained a beacon of hope and inspiration for all who had crossed her path. With unwavering resilience and a heart full of compassion, she transformed not only her own life but the lives of countless others, proving that with determination and courage, anything was possible. Through the grace of her Heavenly Father, Ms. Yu had amassed a fortune beyond her wildest dreams, becoming a millionaire by the age of 40. Her life after 40 can be appreciated by reading the other biography I wrote of her son's life " I'm not Chinese, I'm English! A Singaporean Living with Language Disorder"

And so, as she reflected on her journey from humble beginnings to unimaginable success, Ms. Yu couldn't help but marvel at the twists and turns in her career that had led her to this moment. From walking the depressing hallways of prison and military camps, and the noisy hallways of many different schools, to jetting about in Business and First Class Cabins, hers was a story of resilience, determination, and the unwavering belief that anything was possible with faith and perseverance. This concludes Mrs Yu's Made in Singapore, Rags to Riches Story.

In the words of Mrs Yu

Many a tale has been spun about the pursuit of wealth, the quest to amass one's first million dollars by the age of 30. It's a narrative often painted with strokes of investments in stocks, properties, gold, and bullion. But for many who embark on this journey, the path to riches is often paved with privilege, their pockets lined with the inheritance of old wealth.

Yet, amidst the glitz and glamour, there lies a darker truth. For too many, the sudden influx of wealth proves to be a double-edged sword, a burden too heavy to bear. They succumb to the temptations of excess, drowning their sorrows in booze and drugs, their lives spiraling into chaos and despair.

But for me, my story unfolds from a different vantage point, one rooted in faith and humility. I trace my journey not to ancestral riches or trust funds but to the boundless grace of my Heavenly Father, the Creator of Heaven and Earth. In His eyes, I am indeed a trust fund kid, the beneficiary of His divine providence.

Every opportunity, every blessing that has come my way, I attribute to God alone. I did not chart this course through sheer willpower or ambition; rather, I surrendered to the guidance of a higher power, allowing His wisdom to illuminate my path.

To be entrusted with such abundance is both a blessing and a burden, for I am keenly aware of the responsibility that accompanies it. My Heavenly Father calls upon me to be a steward of His resources, to utilize them wisely for the betterment of His Kingdom on earth.

Though the path ahead may be unclear, I place my trust in His divine plan, confident that He will reveal His purpose to me in His own time. And to those who have walked alongside me on this journey, I extend my deepest gratitude, for you are more than friends – you are my brothers and sisters in Christ.

For in the grand tapestry of life, it is not the material wealth we accumulate that defines us, but the lives we touch and the souls we inspire to seek the saving grace of our Lord Jesus Christ. And so, I echo the words of Scripture, "Seek first the Kingdom of God and His righteousness, and all these things will be added unto you." For true wealth lies not in the treasures of this world, but in the eternal promise of salvation that awaits those who profess Jesus is God.

As I reflect on my journey, I am reminded of the countless blessings that have shaped my path. From the humble beginnings of my childhood to the heights of success I have achieved, each step has been guided by the hand of my Heavenly Father.

Growing up in a modest household, I learned the value of hard work and perseverance from a young age. My parents instilled in me a strong work ethic and a deep sense of gratitude for the blessings we had. They may not have been wealthy in material terms, but they were rich in love and faith, and that was more than enough.

As I ventured out into the world, I faced my fair share of challenges and setbacks. There were times when it seemed like success was out of reach, and the road ahead was fraught with obstacles. But through it all, I clung to my faith, trusting in God's plan for my life.

And then, against all odds, doors began to open, opportunities presented themselves, and blessings poured forth in abundance. From my career to my family to my finances, every aspect of my life was touched by God's grace.

But with great blessings came great responsibility. I knew that I was not meant to hoard my wealth or cling to it selfishly. Instead, I was called to be a vessel of God's love and generosity, using my resources to uplift others and advance His Kingdom on earth.

So I embarked on a journey of giving, supporting charitable causes, and lending a helping hand to those in need. Whether it was providing for the less fortunate, offering a listening ear to those in despair, or sharing the message of God's love with others, I sought to be a beacon of hope and light in a world filled with darkness.

As I look back on my life, I am filled with gratitude for all that I have been given and all that I have been able to give in return. For true wealth is not measured in material possessions or earthly treasures, but in the love we share, the lives we touch, and the legacy we leave behind.

In the end, it is not the size of our bank accounts or the value of our assets that matters, but the impact we have on the world and the souls we lead to salvation. And so, I thank my Heavenly Father for His boundless blessings and His unwavering love, and I pray that He will continue to guide me on this journey of faith and service for all the days of my life.

Matthew 16:26 " For what will it profit a man if he gains the whole world and forfeits his soul?